# CAMPING WITH BABIES AND TODDLERS

OVER 100 TIPS FOR MAKING FAMILY CAMPING
FUN AND EASY

## KIRSTEN FRASER OLDREAD

## ABOUT THE AUTHOR

Kirsten Fraser Oldread is an Outdoor Educator, adventurer, and mama to a young son and toddler daughter. She is the director of a forest school for children in the Colorado mountains. She is a former ski instructor and ski patroller, wilderness EMT, and sailor. Find out more at www. theadventuremama.com.

❄

# CONTENTS

# LET'S GO CAMPING!

*Let's DO THIS!*

S o, you want to go camping with your kids. Hit the open road. Make family memories. Post fun pictures on FB and Instagram.

But does the thought of everything you need to

do just to leave the house have you feeling over-whelmed? I'd love to help.

I'm Kirsten Fraser Oldread. I'm an Outdoor Educator and mother. I know the benefits of spending time in nature with your kids (not to mention yourself) firsthand. I've spent years of nights sleeping under the stars and have learned a few unique tips for camping with toddlers and babies along my path to motherhood. It wasn't always pretty and it's definitely not always easy, but it is ALWAYS worth it to get outside with my kids. For their sake. For mine.

But first, this guide is **NOT** for you if you're looking for an off-the-beaten-path, backcountry backpacking adventure.

This guide **IS** for you if you're looking to spend a weekend or a week under the stars, roasting marshmallows by the fire, car camping with your young family, making memories that you'll treasure for the rest of your lives.

Before we begin... You've presumably logged some nights in a tent already. You know how special a night spent under the stars is, with a campfire to warm your body and friends sitting around it telling stories to warm your soul.

Now you've got a kid. Or more than one. And you don't want to give up the things you used to do that made you feel alive. But things are different now.

And that's okay.

You may find yourself needing to let go of some of your expectations of how things used to be. To readjust your priorities. You may not be going out on epic bike rides, but instead enjoying some quiet time around camp, hoping for an epic nap. Your hiking goal may not be trying to log as many miles as you can, or reaching that remote waterfall — but may instead be a half mile (and half-day) meander. Honestly, sometimes we don't even leave camp — instead enjoying exploring the minutiae of our surroundings. I hope that you find the beauty in that, too — in exploring and seeing the world through the eyes of your children. It's one of the most special things in my life, and I hope you love it as much as I do.

# LEAVE NO TRACE

*Beautiful now - beautiful later!*

*B*efore we delve into my most trusted tips and tricks, let's start with the seven Leave No Trace Principles {also known as LNT}, so we can care for our wild places like we care for our children — and protect them, so our children can take *their* children camping one day.

PRINCIPLE 1 - PLAN AHEAD AND PREPARE.

- Know where you're going and how long you'll stay. Know where you can get water and what sort of bathroom situation you'll have. (Also, know your children and what they're comfortable with.)

- Know who you're traveling with. Discuss who does what chores or jobs and areas that you need more support or help. Some people are just not cooks and adding in a camp stove might push their kitchen skills over the edge. I *love* to eat, so for me it's not worth it to force a bad cook to take on that role for the sake of equality — personally, I'd rather do more cooking (and fewer dishes, please!) and make sure my meals are tasty and nourishing.

- Know your local risks and hazards — are you in an area where you're likely to get sunburned? Is there poison ivy? Might you encounter lightning? What type of wildlife are in the area and are they aggressive? Are you at risk for hypothermia or frostbite or heat stroke? Find out the local weather forecast. Have a map of the area if you'll be hiking, biking, or otherwise exploring — don't trust that your phone will work. (I really can't stress this enough.)

- Also, leave an itinerary with someone. This is definitely the professional side of me speaking, I've never had to use an emergency contact or plan, but I always feel better having someone know where I'm going and when to expect me back.

## PRINCIPLE 2 - TRAVEL AND CAMP ON DURABLE SURFACES

- We all love to find that special place where we feel like we have that little corner all to ourselves, but please don't do it at the cost of impacting the environment. There are some really fragile and beautiful places to see — let's make sure our grandchildren's grandchildren can see them, too.

- Drive on established roads. Camp in established campsites. Hike on established trails.

- Ask yourself how you can make the least impact on your beautiful surroundings.

- When the trail is muddy, due to heavy rain or snowmelt, your choices are to stay on the muddy trail or turn back. Do not go off trail, damaging tender plants and flowers — evaluate when it's less impactful to turn around.

- The junction where two ecosystems (like the bank where a forest meets a river, for example) are teeming with organisms, thus need extra care and minimizing of your impact.

# PRINCIPLE 3 - DISPOSE OF WASTE PROPERLY

- Any garbage or uneaten food should be packed out.

- Toilet paper, *both used and unused* should be packed out.

- Poop should either be buried at least 6 inches deep or carried out (diapers, "wag bags", and any other poop bags or disposal methods).

- Rivers are not a washing machine to do your laundry.

- Grey water (used water, including soapy water, that does not contain food particles or fecal matter) should be disposed of 200 yds from a water source.

- Tooth brushing should be sprayed ("broadcast") or spit in a campfire — not spit on the ground.

- Soap should be used sparingly and dishwater sumped (strained) before broadcasting or disposing it on a campfire.

## PRINCIPLE 4 - LEAVE WHAT YOU FIND

- "Take only pictures, keep only memories, leave only footprints"

- Kids are natural thing finders (not to mention picker-uppers) it's how they learn about the world around them. I'm happy to have my children pick up whatever sticks and rocks they want to carry along the way, but we leave what we found at the trailhead before finishing our hike. I offer to take any photos to remember whatever special thing it was.

*Even simple vegetation can seem exciting!*

## PRINCIPLE 5 - MINIMIZE CAMPFIRE IMPACT

- Burning campfires is a great way to enjoy each other's company in the evening, or prepare a meal if you're feeling like Bear Grylls, but they can scar the earth if you don't take measure to protect it. Many areas have become degraded by the overuse of fires and over-harvesting of firewood. Camp stoves have become increasingly dependable and efficient and have become an essential piece of equipment for minimum impact camping. Not to mention that they operate in almost any weather condition!

- Don't bring firewood from home; plan on buying some nearby, and don't harvest wood from the area around your campsite. If you find yourself making a campfire while backpacking, collect wood from 50 feet or so outside of camp and work outwards from there. Only collect "dead and downed" wood.

- Use an existing campfire ring or fire pan to prevent scorching the rocks or burning vegetation on the ground. For a fire pan, you can use an oil pan, grill pan, or the lid of a metal trash can with 3 inch sides propped above the ground on rocks.

- Find out if there's any fire danger in your area and whether or not there are any bans or restrictions during your visit and if you need a permit. Contact the local agency that oversees your camping destination for more information.

- Plan on using a stove to prepare most of your meals. Cooking over the campfire can be fun on occasion, but cooking on a stove is more reliable: cooking food evenly and dependably through all types of weather.

- **Never** leave a fire unattended.

- Make sure all fires are completely extinguished before leaving them unattended.

- Have one adult in charge of the stove or fire to oversee safety with young children.

## PRINCIPLE 6 - RESPECT WILDLIFE

- Don't feed the animals. Don't touch the animals. Don't leave food out that animals can get to. Don't disturb nests or poke holes or otherwise disturb the homes of animals. We are guests in their neighborhood! Let's be considerate.

- Observe at a distance, without frightening the animals or causing them to scatter, {bear country, aside, where it's better to let them know you're around and not to startle them..}

- Do not disturb the plant or animal in your observation. Especially rare, endangered, or otherwise protected species.

- Don't impede or otherwise interfere with a water source. Camp 200 feet away from any water. Don't overuse or contaminate water sources in limited water areas, like the desert or drought locations. Avoid water sources at night when wildlife may use it.

- Store food securely. The requirements for this vary — in some locations you may be able to store your food in a cooler or a vehicle, whereas in other areas this might be very dangerous. Check with your area's local agency to find out best practices.

- If you see any injured or sick animals, notify the local game warden.

- Keep your pet on a leash.

## PRINCIPLE 7 - BE COURTEOUS TO OTHER VISITORS

- If you want to listen to music, wear headphones or keep the volume turned down if you're using a speaker at camp. Your neighbors might not be into joining your Madonna / Bon Jovi dance party.

- Keep track of your pet. Keep them leashed or otherwise contained, so they don't disturb other camps or wildlife. Pick up all droppings and uneaten food.

- When passing someone on the trail, step off the trail on the downhill side. Downhill traffic yields to uphill traffic, bikers yield to hikers and runners, and everyone yields to horses.

- When you're passing, approach the party slowly, announce your presence politely and when the time comes to pass, do so cautiously.

*If you're interested in learning more straight from the source, check out https://lnt.org/learn/7-principles.*

# CHOOSING A CAMPSITE

*This looks like a good place, Mama!*

𝒶 s the place you're going to call home for your trip, choosing a good campsite is the first step to having a great trip.

- Use established campsites when available. You can find many Forest Service campgrounds and book online at www.recreation.gov, other commercial campgrounds can usually be found using an online search in your destination, as well.

- If there are no established campsites at your ideal destination, make sure your campsite is at least 1/4 mile off of any trails or roads — it's best when your camp can't be seen by any passers by.

- Also ensure you camp 200 yards or more away from any water sources.

- If there is no water at or near your campsite, bring your own in a reusable plastic jug.

- Find an already cleared or impacted spot.

- Look for a site that has even ground.

## COOKING AND EATING

*Food is even more delicious outdoors!*

ood is easily the most important part of camping, hunger can make all the wheels fall off the bus. {True story — once we blew a tire on the way to get dinner while we were camping in Moab. It wasn't fun.} Eating enough of the right foods will help you sleep warmer and deeper through the night. {More sleeping tips later on.} I have seen some of the toughest of leaders crumble to food stress. {It's even happened to me...}

## PROPER FOOD STORAGE

First, store your food properly to protect both your family and wildlife. If you need any guidance on local regulations, call the governing agency for your destination.

## HANDWASHING CAN SAVE YOUR TRIP!

Wash hands or use hand sanitizer before preparing and eating all food. While I fall hard into the "anti-hand sanitizer" camp when we're at home and stand firmly into the "it's healthy for my child to eat dirt" side of the argument, when I'm out camping I'm adamant about hand washing prior to eating. You would be too, if you've seen a foodborne illness or stomach bug rip through an entire group in the middle of the woods on a multiple-week course, miles in from from the nearest trailhead.

Keeping hands clean is the best way to prevent all illness: foodborne, bacterial, viral and fecal.

- To wash hands with hot water and soap {without scalding yourself}, fill a nalgene (or other heat safe) bottle 1/2 with cold water and 1/2 with boiled water. Unscrew the lid halfway and tip to pour, keeping one hand on the lid so it doesn't fall off and douse the handwasher. Don't forget to scrub under your fingernails!

- I like to have a mesh bag with a small bottle of castile soap and a nail brush that I keep with the hand washing station. I don't use the nail brush every time, but like to keep it on hand for when the kids (or adults) need a solid scrub down.

- Another great option for a handwashing station (among other uses) we really like is NEMO Equipment's Helio, an air pressurized, portable camp shower with a kitchen sprayer nozzle.

- Wash hands away from camp or over an extinguished fire ring. This minimizes the impacts of soap and the leftover charcoal and ashes from the fire does a great job filtering the grey water.

*Only grownups in the kitchen.*

## COOKING AND SAFETY

- Have a separate kitchen area, away from the general flow of traffic and away from your sleeping area.

- Cook only on a stable surface — the ground or a flat boulder are best. There's not much worse than spilled dinner, except a spilled dinner that burns someone. That can ruin your trip pretty quickly.

- Cook up high off the ground, if possible — but keep in mind what my dad always said, "Things can't fall up." Stability takes priority over height. Make sure you're cooking out of high traffic areas and not at a knock-able height.

- Only cooks are allowed in the kitchen, whether you're taller or shorter than three feet. It's best to keep everyone out of the kitchen, to maximize child coverage and reduce potential spills and mix ups.

- Start preparing dinner a little earlier than usual — it's probably going to take longer than to usual to prepare. You know, like everything with kids and new environments.

- To stave off any dinner time meltdowns have a protein snack while preparing — we love veggies and hummus, rolled up cold cuts, or cheese sticks.

- For bottle fed babies, powder based formula is easier than liquid — less storage is required and no refrigeration needed!

- Consider bringing extra bottles, so you don't have to worry about sanitizing with every feeding. Plan on enough for 1-2 days, if possible.

- To warm the bottle, fill a mug with boiling water and set the bottle inside. (I was well warned by another mama that using a mason jar in cold weather may result in a cracked jar when the hot water was added. Now you're warned, too.) For middle of the night feedings, boiling water ahead of time and putting it in a vacuum sealed thermos can help keep the process efficient.

- For early eaters, bring homemade mashes prepared in small, 1-2 portion sized containers. Or refillable pouches, if you use them.

- For dinners, we go with easy to prepare, least common denominator foods — mac and cheese with peas or broccoli, tortellini or other pasta, pre-cooked sausage and veggies, or burgers — and some ready-made salad in a bag for the parents. Also, the quicker the cooking time, the better. We're not afraid to bring pre-cooked meals (read: leftovers) to reheat, instead of making a meal — especially if it was already a big hit at home.

- Bring familiar favorites for meals. While gado-gado sauce may be one of my favorite camping dinner flavors, I can't expect my toddler to dive into something new and different with joy and enthusiasm, while in a completely new and possibly challenging environment. Instead, I pack the tortellini he loves and slather them with extra butter. Because butter might be one of his food groups. {But maybe that's just my kid...} ; )

- For breakfasts, we often bring easy meals like muffins and yogurt or kefir and a special juice or instant oatmeal. And hot cocoa of course.

- Lunches are usually snacks, fruit, veggie sticks, and tortilla roll-ups — food that packs easy and can be held in one hand and eaten. I like to make them in the morning, so we can go on an adventure whenever we're ready.

- Butter makes everything better — the more the merrier!

- Bring other, more flavorful sauces for adults to add to meals on their own plates.

- Save leftovers in a ziplock plastic bag for lunch the next day.

- Bring a few more snacks than you think you'll need.

- It's entirely possible that your kid will be so distracted with their surroundings, that they will lose interest in eating — it's not worth fighting a food battle with them. No one will die from a weekend (or even a week) of eating just pb&j's or cheese sticks.

- Conversely, it's also possible that their metabolism will be so revved by the day's explorations and experiences that they might be ravenous. If your child hasn't eaten a big dinner or has been running their head off all day and you're worried that they might wake up hungry, bring a snack to bed with you (aggressive bear areas aside, obviously know where you're going, use your judgment and prioritize your family's safety...) Outside of bear territory, I often bring a piece of fruit like an apple, pear or banana, a drink box of milk or juice, or something in a package like cheese sticks, fruit chews, or a granola bar.

## OUTDOOR DINING

- Sitting: A collapsible high chair, a bath seat on the ground, a bumbo chair, or a clamp on seat if there is a picnic table — options depend on age and mobility. A child's sized camp chair and a cooler, storage box, or milk crate turned on its side are a great table and chair for toddlers and preschoolers.

*Camp chairs come in child sizes.*

- Plastic bibs with a trough work great -
  they catch the food before it hits the
  ground (less clean up later) and can be
  easily wiped clean.

- Bring 1 bandanna or cloth napkin per
  day to wipe face and hands and leave it
  tied onto the baby's seat. Use for the day
  and place it in the wash.

EASY CLEAN UP

- Use a mild, unscented, all-purpose castile
  soap like Dr Bronner's for washing up.

- After washing up, strain the dirty wash water through a mesh sieve to collect any food particles. Pour the dirty water into campfire ring or "broadcast" it. If you're unfamiliar, broadcasting is a way to disperse your strained grey water, toothpaste spit, or other food-smelling/animal-attracting wastewater—usually spraying it, as opposed to dumping it in one place. Place strained food particles in the trash and pack it out when you leave.

- To sterilize your plates, cups, bottles, and utensils dip them in a pot of boiling water. I do this every or every other day, depending on meals and time.

# 5

# PEEING AND POOPING

*Potty chairs can go anywhere!*

$\mathcal{W}$hile probably not too different than at home, depending on what stage your child is at, hygiene is really important when you're out in the woods. Make sure you bring adequate hand sanitizer.

- Plan ahead and prepare — know your bathroom situation: is there a flush toilet? A long drop? Will you be digging cat holes or using wag-bags? Talk about this with your child prior to your trip. If your child is still in diapers, get an average of how many they use in a day.

- Bring extra diapers, underwear, pull-ups, and wipes! Even if your kid has been potty trained for a while. And wipes, did I mention bring lots of wipes?

- Pick out a designated pee area, prior to needing it, outside of camp and introduce it to your child. Familiarize them to it, maybe have them pick out a plant or rock to pee on. Or **not** pee on, if there's poison ivy, oak or sumac around! (Or a wasp's nest — they are definitely not fun to pee on.)

- Your child may need a little prompting and guidance on going for the first couple of times. Ask them frequently at the beginning and be prepared for some accidents.

- Dog poop bags are my best friend. Can't make it in time to dig a hole or out to the privy? Have your child poop into the bag or onto the ground and pick it up.

- Hang a trash bag for diapers. We use a tree branch or side view mirror, depending on the campsite.

- Bring a wet bag or some extra plastic or ziplock bags or for any accidents on clothes.

- Tell your children when you're going to the bathroom. Even better, take them with you.

- Have a privy kit ready. Include a diaper, wipes, poop bag, toilet paper, hand sani, and a trowel. We like to keep ours in a small stuff sack in the side pocket of the passenger door. Everyone knows where it is and can tell by its absence if someone is already using it; plus it has everything you need.

- Mamas, if you are in the phase of life where you or your daughter might get your period, I like to have a small toiletries bag filled with all my preferred necessities. I keep this with the privy kit.

- If there is going to be a "long-drop" or vault toilet your child may feel more comfortable using a potty-seat insert.

- Or you can have them place their feet on the seat and squat. This is a pants off first and lots of holding maneuver. Putting them in the squatting position makes it a more ergonomic pooping position - easier for everything to come out, if they have been holding or haven't been able to go. Be aware that the exit directions for pee and poop may not be the same angle, you may want the to try peeing first.

- It's not uncommon to have your child (or other adults) hold their poop in. Talk about why it's important for your body to eliminate. Also, make sure they're getting enough water and fluids. Holding in poop can lead to constipation and drinking enough can help prevent stool from becoming hard and difficult to eliminate. If you're concerned that your child might do this, bringing along a can of prune juice can help.

- Some families just bring a little potty and empty / wipe it out. One with a lid is best.

- Bring an extra pair or two of medical gloves for cleaning up a mess, especially when you don't have as good access to hand washing as you do at home.

PRIVY KIT PACKING LIST

- 1 small stuff sack
- 1 roll of toilet paper in a ziplock plastic bag
- hand sanitizer
- trowel
- diaper
- wipes
- (dog) poop bag
- 1- 2 pair nitrile gloves, stored inside a zip top plastic bag
- 2 extra ziplock bags *optional

# 6

# PLAYING

*Some toys are perfect in camp!*

*E*very family has their own strategy on what to bring and play with when you're out camping. Here are some helpful strategies we've used and we've seen other families implement.

- We love to bring sand toys — a shovel and bucket are great toys for camping.

- Bring fewer toys than you think — bring a couple of outdoor favorites, but when in doubt leave it out.

- Some people bring no toys and let their kids fully immerse themselves in nature.

- Some families bring an extra tent to use as a kids play zone. Books and special toys can be used inside, kids can get some shade and have a special play area for themselves. {Best of all, sand can stay out of your sleeping tent!}

- Set aside a play area boundary. This can also include areas to avoid like water sources, kitchen, campfire, etc.

- Talk about any hazards they may encounter — insects, snakes, plants, vehicles, water sources, bugs or animals to be aware of.

- It's ok to pick up plants, flowers, and sticks from the ground, but it's not okay to pick or break off living ones. And make sure you have the discussion about what not to eat or plants not to touch, like poison ivy!

- Leave what you find when you're done playing with it — don't take home your new pet rock collection, leave it for others to enjoy. We like to take pictures of any special rocks and sticks that we're having trouble leaving behind.

- Brush away any remnants of play that happened — make it look like you weren't there.

- Make cleaning up fun. We like to play clean up bingo: "I'm looking for a blue bucket", or whatever you have, repeat until cleaned up…

- Bomb-proof your camp at night and anytime you leave. Having a bucket, large tupperware box, or bag can be helpful for corralling toys.

# 7

## TENTS AND SLEEPING

*I love our tent, Mama!*

*E*asily the second most important {or do I mean stressful?} part about camping — we're talking 'bout Maslow's hierarchy of needs, people! It's all about finding what works for your family and setting yourself up for success. It's worth it to invest some time into choosing a good location to set up your home away from home, aka your tent.

- Find a spot away from the campfire and the kitchen to set up your tent. Flat, rockless spots without vegetation are ideal.

- If you're using dispersed camping or otherwise not in a designated campsite, make sure your tent and campsite are at least 200 yards away from any water sources and at least 1/4 mile off of any trails or roads.

- No playing in the tent — tents are for sleeping only. This will help keep your sleeping bags sand, dirt, and grit free.

- Get changed right away, when you get up; PJ stay clean and ready for bed. (We often skip getting dressed and ride home in our PJs on the last day, though.)

- To have some ambient light in the tent at night, hang a headlamp or other non-flammable lantern from the tent ceiling. Most tents have something on the ceiling, like a gear hammock, attachment hook, vent, or zipper pull that you can affix your headlamp to. We like the efficiency and small size of a collapsible solar LED lantern.

- Keep shoes out of the tent. Take them off and leave them upside down in the vestibule. Give them a shake in the morning before putting them on to make sure no critters have used them for shelter.

- Make sure to sleep with your heads uphill, if you're on an incline.

- New sleeping areas can be challenging for some children. Plan on going in the tent early to familiarize them.

- Keep a few tent-only toys and books for special {ahem, early rising} mornings and before bedtime.

- Bring in an easy snack for morning that doesn't make a mess or spill. Apples or a granola bar are our top picks. *This tip is obviously location dependent — make sure you plan ahead and prepare. If you're camping in an aggressive bear area, use appropriate precautions, including keeping food out of tents.*

## WHAT TO DO AT BEDTIME

- Putting toddlers and babies to bed can be difficult, because of the new environment. One strategy is to have a parent plan on going to bed when the kid(s) go to bed. You can trade off.

- If that doesn't work, letting the kids stay up until the parents are ready to go to bed (or the kid completely melts down) are also acceptable options. Some kids will be able to put themselves to sleep, but being in a new, stimulating, and unfamiliar environment, this isn't always the case.

- Don't forget to bring pillows! You don't need to rough it that much! :)

- Your child is probably burning more calories from a day of new adventures (and maybe a missed nap) If they wake up in the night / melt down before bed, consider checking in to see if they need an extra snack before bed. *Again, plan ahead and prepare — know if bears are a danger where you'll be camping and use your best judgment.*

HOW TO DRESS FOR BED

- Toddler sleep scenario, in a sleeping bag: long johns or bodysuit, fleece footie pajamas or fleece pants (if needed), fleece jacket, mittens, hat, puffy jacket (if needed), wool socks (underneath pajamas, if needed and there's enough room). I find that my toddler flips and flops throughout the night — sometimes he's in and sometimes he's out. Having a fleece jacket or puffy jacket on him if it's

really cold can help him stay warm when
he's out of the bag.

- Baby Snowsuit Sleep system: Bodysuit,
  fleece footie pajamas (depending on the
  season), fleece or down bunting, mittens
  (if needed), hat that ties under the chin,
  booties or socks under their PJs (if
  needed).

- Please use your best judgment and be
  vigilant about protecting your baby's
  airway. Keep sleeping bags and other
  blankets and jackets away from your
  baby's face, to prevent suffocation.

- If very cold for baby (and there's room in
  the bunting) take their arms out of the
  sleeves and tuck them against their torso.

# 8

## STAYING AND SLEEPING WARM

*Woodland elves are everywhere!*

$\mathcal{A}$ cold, sleepless night can easily ruin the next day or your whole trip. But just because it's cold out, doesn't mean that you have to feel cold while you sleep! Having appropriately rated equipment should be your first step to sleeping warm - there's not very much you can do to stay toasty if you bring a 40 degree rated sleeping bag when the temps drop to -10. A mummy style bag also helps keep you warmer, by covering your head and eliminating drafts around your neck.

There are two important parts of staying warm. First is stoking your internal fire by eating fat, calorie and nutrient dense foods. The next step is to move your core muscles to generate heat.

## HOW TO SLEEP WARM

- Take a snack to bed. *Again, not always an acceptable option in aggressive bear country (plan ahead and prepare, know your local risk factors),* but this will definitely get your metabolic fire stoked and elevate your body temperature if you are feeling chilly in the middle of the night.

- High fat foods will "burn" for longer, keeping you warmer through the night.

- Also, getting up to pee in the middle of the night can help you sleep warmer. Your body doesn't have to spend energy keeping your pee warm if your bladder is empty.

- Go to bed warm: get your blood moving and your heart beating if you're feeling cold from being too sedentary. A sleeping bag is like a thermos — if you put something warm in there, it will stay warm. But if you put something cold in there, it will remain cold. I like to go for a little run, have a dance party or do some jumping jacks at night when I'm really cold — not so much that you break a sweat, just enough to warm your bones.

- If I wake up cold, and peeing and eating haven't warmed me up, the next step is exercise. Doing push ups or sit ups in your sleeping bag can get your large muscles firing and your blood flowing.

- Don't wear so many layers that you think you might be Ralphie's little brother from "A Christmas Story." Insulation needs air space to trap the heat. Just not too much space that you have a draft! (It's a delicate balance.)

- Although it may be cold outside, having your tent vented by leaving windows and doors open will prevent condensation (from your breathing and body temperature). True even in winter, though you don't need to have every vent fully opened when it's really cold outside.

- Putting on the rain fly will also help your tent retain some heat.

- Air mattresses with foam inside them (like Thermarests) or closed cell foam pads (like Ridge Rests) will keep you much warmer than a big air mattress. This is because air doesn't do a good job of insulating. Foam pads tend to be less comfortable than inflatable ones.

- Wearing a hat to bed can help you sleep much warmer. Your body loses a lot of heat from your head.

- The warmer you eat, the warmer you'll sleep. High-calorie and high-fat foods provide your body with longer burning fuel to keep you warm throughout the night.

- Having a sleeping bag that's too long can make your feet cold. (Really, really cold.) If your sleeping bag is too big for you, take up a little extra space around the feet by stuffing a jacket or other piece of clothing at the bottom. Like we talked about before, just don't make it too tight!

- Sleeping with your face and mouth inside your sleeping bag, while it may feel cozy at first, will eventually accumulate moisture and make you colder. Use a mummy style sleeping bag and cinch it down around the top of your head and neck.

- Wearing a neck warmer to sleep can help keep you feeling toasty if the weather is cold.

- Keep a pair of loose-fitting sleeping socks at the bottom of your sleeping bag, instead of wearing sweaty ones you had on during the day. My favorite is a hand knit pair a friend made for me!

# 9

# NAPS

*Exciting day - let's nap!*

$\mathcal{N}$apping can be one of the trickiest parts of camping with young ones and every child's ideal sleep scenario is different. If your child is a strict, only can fall asleep in their crib with blackout curtains and a white noise machine going type of child, this may be your biggest challenge and you may prefer to wait until they're a little more flexible or phasing out of naps. If you're up for an adventure, here are some strategies that may help.

- Midday tent use can be really hot. Find a shady spot to pitch your tent with this in mind or shade your tent with a tarp. When napping, open all windows and vent all doors, also consider taking the rainfly off — weather dependent, of course.

- Sometimes there is a romper room effect that happens, as a toddler gives up their last hurrah before allowing themself to fall into sleep. Having a few books, a stuffy, and an enclosed space to stay reined in help contain this waning energy.

- Nap in a stroller. If you're in an area where you can push a stroller and that is comfortable and soothing for your child, try that.

- Nap in a backpack or baby carrier. Pick a hiking destination that will allow for some pre-nap distance (and maybe some pre-nap exploring to tucker them out) and some napping mileage. Keep in mind, your little adventurer might be more stimulated if this isn't their norm, so it may take longer for them to fall asleep.

- Nap in the car. Plan a destination — scenic drive or adventure with a nap-length drive. Or at least a drive that will initiate the napping sequence, if not last the entire length. (I've definitely arrived at trailheads, parked, and read a book because my toddler fell asleep on the way, though it's easier if this happens on the way back.)

- Napping in the back of your truck? We have a pickup truck with a topper and often times sleep there with the windows open. It's otherwise similar to sleeping in a tent.

- Naps may be shorter than usual, which may or may not make for an easier bedtime...

# 10

# DRESSING AND CLOTHING

*You know it's an adventure if you're wearing a cowboy hat!*

$\mathcal{D}$ressing for camping doesn't have to include a set of special clothes, but plan on bringing items that you don't mind getting dirty. And expect to run them through a heavy duty cycle wash cycle when you get home. There are a few special items like a good base layer and warm wool socks that can make everyone more comfortable and the trip more enjoyable.

- Have a set of PJs to wear in the tent only. Change into regular clothes for the day before leaving the tent. We often use long johns as PJs, but synthetic footie PJs are great, too.

- Dress in layers: base, insulating, and outer / element protection — remove or add, as needed.

- Base layer keeps you warm when wet {sweat, drool, potty accident, you know...}

- Insulation layer is usually fleece, but might also be wool or down (if you're not worried about wetness)

*Cozy fleece keeps baby comfy on a cold morning.*

- Element protection is a windbreaker or rain jacket, if it's well, you know. If it might rain.

- Have a pair of clean, dry, wool socks for the night. Smartwool are the easiest brand to find for toddlers and babies.

- Wear a sunhat during the day and winter hats at night, if it's cold.

- Polypropylene, Capilene, or wool base layers are great for keeping kids warm if they get wet from a potty accident / playing in water — AND they dry quickly!

- We use well-loved hand-me-downs and thrift stores finds for clothing and outerwear while camping and save their nice clothes and jackets for home.

# 11

## PACKING AND ORGANIZING

*Our typical truckbed organization*

*H*ave a system and stick with it. {Unless it's not working, then reassess.} I wish I could tell you *exactly* what to do, but everyone has different space / equipment needs. Here are some things that work for us.

- If one parent is better at organization than the other, let them take the lead. It's helpful for both parents to understand the organization system, though — so you don't work against each other.

- It works best with our space to pack almost everything into Rubbermaid boxes. We have a sleeping bag box, a sleeping pad and pillow duffle bag, a kitchen box, and food boxes. The best part about using boxes with lids is that they can be left outside if it rains.

- Tape a checklist of each box's inventory to the lid or write it directly on the box.

*Rubbermaid boxes also make perfect tables!*

## KITCHEN BOX SUPPLIES:

1. plates
2. bowls
3. mugs
4. cutlery
5. cutting knife
6. cutting board
7. fry pan
8. pot
9. serving spoon
10. spatula
11. paper towels
12. corkscrew / bottle opener

13. lighter(s)
14. stove top espresso maker or inexpensive French press (Ikea has great, inexpensive ones!)
15. can opener
16. Don't forget your stove and fuel!

## CLOTHES

- Use either ziplock plastic bags or stuff sacks to keep like items together. Some folks prefer to put each outfit into their own ziplock. I don't have time or patience for that level of organization, so I just group like things together: socks and undies, shirts, pants. Outerwear gets stuffed in their duffle without a bag. PJs get stuffed into pillowcases in the morning.

- I like to tuck an extra stuff sack for dirty laundry in each person's bag. It makes it easier to grab a clean change of clothes as you need it and unpacking / doing laundry is a synch!

- When I'm at camp and going in and out of bags, I like to place everyone's on the floor of the car, by their respective seats or in their carseat. I know where to find whoever's stuff I need and it's out of the way while we're stationary.

- When we pack up to go on a day's adventure, we just move all bags to the trunk or leave them in the tent.

## ORGANIZATION SYSTEMS ... AND THE "WHOOPS" FACTOR

- Organization systems will need to be constantly re-organized and put back into place. This may take more time than you expect. I like to buzz around at night before bed and make sure everything is in place again so I know where to find all of our things.

- Do you have that one thing you always forget? Mine is my headlamp (though I've been known to forget a down jacket while heading to the snowy mountains, too, whoops!). I write myself extra notes so I don't forget these things, I put my headlamp in my toiletries kit, and I've got a spare (one for the toddler.) Hindsight is 20/20 in this case, but take a moment to think about what items you are likely to forget or have forgotten (perhaps frequently) in the past or that you would really, really hate to leave behind. Make a checklist of these items. Double check that list before driving away.

# CHOOSE YOUR OWN ADVENTURE

*Who needs toys when there are rocks and a stream?!*

ow it's your turn! Hopefully, you're feeling inspired and prepared to head out on the open road and find your own family adventure under a starry sky somewhere. So grab the marshmallows, pack up the car and get out there, have fun, and make memories with your family that will last a lifetime. **And don't forget your headlamp!**

- And if you post any pics on Instagram, tag me so I can see what you're up to. And follow along with my family's adventures and any new tips and tricks we figure out along the way instagram.com/theadventuremama.

- If sharing pics of your family on social media isn't your thing, you can always reach me at mama@theadventuremama.com.

Happy adventures!
~Kirsten

Printed in Great Britain
by Amazon

19553239R00048